SEE

WITH

YOUR

EARS

First published in 1983 by
Lexikos
703 Market Street
San Francisco, California 94103

Designed by Craig Bergquist.
Illustration direction by the author.
Text set in Century Bold with Century
Schoolbook and Avant Garde
by Turner & Brown, Inc.
Printed by Edwards Brothers, Inc.

See With Your Ears—Teacher's Guide,
a 20-page booklet (ISBN
0-938530-20-8), is available directly
from the publisher for $2 plus 50¢
postage and handling.

Manufactured in the United States of
America.

Library of Congress Catalogue Number
82-081463

ISBN 0-938530-09-7

83 84 85 86 87 5 4 3 2 1

SEE WITH YOUR EARS

THE CREATIVE MUSIC BOOK

WRITTEN BY
DON KAPLAN

ILLUSTRATED BY
MARYANNE REGAL HOBURG

LEXIKOS

SAN FRANCISCO

CONTENTS

PART B:

FACING THE MUSIC

PART C:

KNOWING THE SCORE

A NOTE TO ADULTS

After all, it was *good* for you to practice the piano and take violin lessons. Going to a concert gave you instant culture; attending an opera was the height of sophistication. "Serious" music was to be studied and admired and, like anything else that was good for you, it was usually greeted with dread and suspicion.

A child's first music lessons aren't usually very exciting. The names and dates of composers are just something to memorize; notation, something that's enforced without apparent reason. Adults may recognize the value of learning a musical language and history, but children more often find it useless and hardly worth the effort.

What gets lost among the leger lines is the joy of making sounds—the pure pleasure of creating music by yourself and with others. Music has become less accessible than the other arts: you don't have to first learn a system of notation to paint or sculpt or dance. (Of course, you have to learn specific techniques to paint or sculpt or dance *well.*) Music not only requires us to listen (something we do very little of in our visually oriented society), but to listen for extended periods of time (the very thought of which is enough to provoke the fidgets). Even singing can become an obstacle if you have been declared "tone deaf" and sent to the back of the chorus.

Introductory experiences with music that emphasize memorization without motivation can develop negative attitudes that will last a lifetime. *See With Your Ears* is intended to develop positive attitudes toward music. It enables children to experience the creative process without passively relying on recordings or having to study the mechanics of music. Parents and teachers (and anyone else in the company of children) will find engaging ways to introduce musical elements using materials everyone can feel comfortable with. While the activities are arranged sequentially and generally move from simple to complex, many of them can be taught as individual games or puzzles.

Part A of the book focuses on developing listening skills and an awareness of sounds, and on identifying basic elements of sound. *Part B* provides musical resources using sounds children naturally make, and applies them to musical composition. The activities in this section follow the natural evolution of music, enabling youngsters to invent their own musical languages, understand what led to standardized notation, and use sounds in a structured, disciplined way. *Part C* incorporates materials from the preceding sections for composition in a variety of traditional and contemporary formats.

See With Your Ears is written to be used by children—alone, in pairs, and in groups—with a little help from adults. Non-readers will need guidance throughout; older children will be able to work independently after being introduced to the materials. In addition to nourishing creativity and self-expression, the activities will stimulate interest in music as an art and encourage children to study music in its classical forms. Children who are already making music will find new and exciting ways to look at what they are doing. Children without musical experience will be building a foundation from which formal training can begin.

The activities can be done at any time, in any place, with little or no preparation. But a word of warning: music is contagious. Keep this book close at hand or you might miss an opportunity to try some composing and sound-making yourself.

A NOTE TO CHILDREN

Do you ever wonder how people compose
music? Or how they write for all those instruments? Or what it's like to lead an orchestra?
Here's your chance to be a composer, a conductor, and a performer—all rolled into one.
You can write a symphony for scissors, or a
chorus of coughs. You can find melodies in
your name, or paint with your voice. And you
don't have to know a G clef from an F to do it.

Whatever language people speak, music is
something everyone can understand. It's a

way of telling others how we feel, and of feeling good about ourselves. Music develops our minds as well as our ears, and helps us learn more about each other.

Anybody can "see with their ears." Even if you don't know a thing about music, this book will help you discover all kinds of music around you. If you already sing or play an instrument, it will help you enjoy what you are doing even more. You'll find games to play alone. You'll find games to play with a friend or a group of friends. You'll find paper music and talking walls, sound shadows and mystery tours, rib ticklers and "ooblah waah"— and ways to have fun inventing your own compositions.

The best way to use this book is to start at the beginning and go through to the end. Most of the activities in Part A can be done at any time, in any place. The games in Part B get harder as they go along, and should be played in order. Part C combines everything from Parts A and B, so do those parts first. If you can't figure out how to do an activity, draw a sound, or put sounds together, ask an adult for some help.

There's music everywhere, from the screeching of cars to the patter of rain. When you listen to sounds, listen like you never listened before. They are the sounds closest to you, and the material from which music is made.

PART A: SOUND ADVICE

Most people don't listen very carefully. They might hear what you say, but they are often thinking about something else. About what they saw on television. Or what they had for lunch. This isn't something they do on purpose: they just don't know how to listen. And the same thing happens with music.

The games in this part will help you listen to each other and the sounds around you more carefully. They will help you examine what goes into your ears, and to discover some sounds you never heard before. When you play the games, try a few with your eyes closed: that way, you can be sure you are really listening. Besides, sometimes it's more fun to see with your ears instead of your eyes.

FAR AND NEAR

A.1

Right now, listen to everything you can hear outside the room you are in. After a minute or so, write down what you heard. (The longer you listen, the more you'll hear.) Listen a second time for anything you can hear *inside* the room. Again, write down the results.

How many outside sounds were you able to hear? Were you able to hear at least five sounds inside? Some indoor sounds might include people walking and breathing, stomachs rumbling, clocks ticking, fluorescent lights buzzing, paper rustling, floors creaking, clothes rubbing, and faucets dripping. Try this with your parents or friends and see who can hear the most sounds. Listen in the same place, at different times, on the same day. Do you hear the same things? Listen at the same time, in the same place, on another day. Do you still hear the same things?

Try the exercise outdoors, listening first for the sounds furthest away, then for the sounds closest to you. Can you tell which direction they are coming from? Really strengthen your ears: every time you do the exercise, try to find two new sounds you haven't heard before.

VOICE PRINTS

It's easy to see colors on paper. It's harder to *hear* colors, but you can when you know how to listen for them.

If you read this sentence out loud, you will discover your voice has a *volume* (from loud to soft), a *pitch* (high, middle, or low quality), and a *rhythm* (made up of long and short sounds). Your voice also has its own special "color," called *timbre* (pronounced *tamber*). The timbre stays the same whether you are talking, singing, crying, or yelling. If two people said the same word, at the same time, on the same pitch, and at the same volume, their voices would still sound different. When two instruments play the same note, their timbres make them sound different, too.

The combination of these four things— timbre, pitch, volume, and rhythm—make your voice (and every sound) unlike any other. In fact, if it was missing one of these things, your voice might not be heard at all. (Imagine what it would sound like if it didn't have volume. Or didn't take time. Or have a place from high to low.)

Listen to people talk. Do they speak quickly or slowly? Do they speak clearly, or slide words together? How do they breathe? If they have a foreign accent, what makes their voice sound different? Does everyone speak at the same volume? Or with the same rhythm?

How would you describe the sound of your own voice? Bright? Breathy? Rich? Nasal? Go into the bathroom and talk into a corner, or tape record your voice. Does it sound the same?

A WALK

A.3

 Listen to the way people walk. Don't just watch—listen! Some people walk v–e–r–y slowly, others very quickly. Some people always sound like they are late for an appoint-

ment; others walk like they have no place to go. Some heavy people hardly make a noise; some thin people sound like they are angry at the floor. The type of shoes you wear, how quickly you walk, the distance between steps, and how forceful the steps are, all add to the sound of a walk.

Concentrate on your walk. Is it fast, medium, or slow? Do you take long strides or short steps? Do you push down on your heels, or push off from the front of your feet? Do you bounce as you walk, or keep your legs stiff?

Hold a piece of paper so you can write on it while you walk. Start walking, and make a mark for each step you take. Place the marks close together if you walk quickly:

I) \ I ((((\ I (I ((\ \ ) (((I I

and further apart if you walk slowly:

ı ɪ ᛆ ᛁ ı ı ı ɪ ı

If your steps are heavy, draw heavy marks:

§ ≩ ≩ ≩ ≩ ≩ ≩ ≩ ♪ ♪

and draw light marks for light steps:

(((((((((

Since your walk will change depending on how you feel, draw your walk when you are excited, upset, tired, or bored. Draw other people's walks and compare them with your own.

HOW LONG
DOES A SOUND LAST?

A.4

Ring a bell. Any bell. Listen carefully as the sound disappears. How long does it take for the ringing to completely stop?

After a bell is rung, the metal continues to vibrate (move back and forth quickly) for several seconds. The sound does not stop instantly. (What would it sound like if it did?)

As the vibrations slow down, the sound fades... but it might take a lot longer to finish than you think.

If you can't find a bell, gently tap an empty glass with the back of a spoon. What happens if you fill the glass with water to different levels? Which sound lasts the longest?

SOUND
SCAVENGER HUNT

A.5

Find all of the following sounds inside your house:
- A crunchy sound
- A funny sound
- An absolutely awful sound
- A scary sound
- A scratchy sound
- A metallic sound
- A constant buzz
- A constant hum
- A scrape and click sound
- A two-click sound
- A hum and click sound
- A sound that suddenly stops
- A sound that reminds you of how a lemon smells
- A sound that reminds you of your favorite color
- A sound that reminds you of how a corncob feels
- A sound you've never noticed before

THE OUTSIDE

A.6

Go outside and listen for:
- The softest sound you can hear on a noisy street
- The loudest sound you can hear on a quiet street
- A single voice within a crowd
- Sounds you can hear over your head

- Sounds you can hear below your knees
- Sounds you can hear in the sky (if you hear one, can you tell which direction it's moving without looking? If it's not moving, you'd better look to see what it is!)
- Sounds that are made by two objects rubbing against each other
- Sounds that are made by two objects hitting each other
- A sound made by shaking something
- A sound made by something blowing across something else
- A sound made by something being blown into
- A pair of footsteps like your own

SHOUT ABOUT

A.7

Different surfaces have different sounds. You can prove this by yelling at them.

Choose a number from one to nine and yell it—sharp, loud, and fast—at different large objects. Put your mouth one inch away from a window and yell your number at it. (Make sure your neighbors aren't home.) Yell the number at the walls. Yell at a table top. Yell at the back of a chair, or the back of a person. Can you hear the difference? Which surfaces make the sharpest sounds?

SENDING A SOUND
ACROSS THE ROOM

A.8

Stand anyplace in a room. Choose any number or word to say. Without moving your body, send your sound toward the floor so that it hits it but stops there. (Don't let it go into the basement.) Send the sound to the ceiling, but don't let it land on the roof. Send it to each of the four walls. Send the sound to different objects at different distances.

With a group of friends, have everyone stand at different distances and close their eyes. Send a sound to someone. Whoever thinks he has "caught" the sound, says so. If he is wrong, send it again. Have the "catcher" send a sound to someone else.

.FIVE

BECOMING AN
AUDITORY
JOURNALIST

A.9

Some people collect stamps. Some collect sounds.

Write down in a notebook sounds that interest you. One might be the strangest sound you've heard inside school or outside on the street. Another might be the darkest, or the most beautiful sound you've heard. Or the shortest sound you've ever heard, or the longest, or just something you liked.

Write down sounds that tell you to do something (like alarm clocks, sirens, telephones, teakettles that whistle, and coffee pots that perk). Write down sounds that tell you something is happening (like gates opening and closing, screeching brakes, barking dogs, and penalty buzzers on quiz shows).

Make a list of places where you hear music (like at football games, in supermarkets, and in elevators). Make a list of sounds you hear every single day, and how those sounds make you feel.

MYSTERY TOUR

Imagine you have been blindfolded and taken someplace. You hear the following sounds:

water boiling
dishes banging
bacon sizzling

Then:

waves splashing
seagulls calling
foghorns sounding

You would know, in the first example, that you were in a kitchen. Of course, you could hear dishes rattling in a restaurant or lunchroom. But you would only hear this *and* the sounds of water boiling and bacon sizzling if you were in or near a kitchen. If you heard the second combination of sounds, you would probably be at the ocean.

Think of a few places you have been (maybe a zoo, farm, subway, bus, railway station, pond, city street, or amusement park). On an index card, list three sounds that would best identify one of the places. Make a separate

card for each place. While you do this, have a
friend make cards listing the sounds of places
she or he has been to. Take turns picking cards
from each other's decks, and try to guess the
locations.

If you can borrow a cassette recorder, go
back to one of the places and tape enough
sounds so someone will know where it is. Be
sure to include the three most typical sounds.
Play the tape for another person. Can they tell
where you've been?

RADIO PLAYS

People used to listen to the radio and see all kinds of things. With some words and a few well chosen sounds you, too, can make anything happen... any time you want.

First write a story. The story can be read by one person, but it is much more fun to have different characters speak as they do in a play. You can also have a program host introduce the play, talk between acts, and comment at the end.

The sounds and words you choose tell listeners where they are and what's happening. Two or three typical sounds can help identify a place (see A.10). A person's voice print and walk can help paint a picture of that person. The music you choose can help set the mood and location. And don't forget sound effects. Use your voice or found objects (see Part B) to make sounds like squeaky doors (rub a balloon), fire (crumple cellophane), or rain (drop rice onto a tightly stretched piece of paper).

Background noises like rolling thunder, back-firing cars, and footsteps coming or going can add depth to your sounds.

To make things clear, you might want to *tag* characters and *plant* sounds. When you tag a character, someone says her name ("Look! There's Mary!"). When you plant a sound, someone names a sound the listener might have trouble identifying ("Why did you open that umbrella in here? You know it will bring bad luck!").

If you can borrow a cassette recorder, tape the play. Or perform it live at lunchtime over your school's speaker system.

DOUBLE TALK

Have you ever tried to pat your head and rub your stomach at the same time? *Double talk* is almost like that, and just as hard.

Both you and a friend tell each other what you have done so far that day, *at the same time*. Don't be polite. Both of you talk at once. Set a timer so you can stop after a minute or so, then take turns telling each other what the *other* person said.

Did you hear everything your friend told you? Were you able to talk and listen at the same time? Better do this late in the day so you have something to talk about.

MORE DOUBLE TALK

Start talking. Have a friend talk with you, trying to say the same thing at the same time. Since he or she can't know what you are going to say, speak slowly and help your friend follow you.

RHYTHM CLAPS

Clap a short rhythm (using long and short claps) and have a friend clap it back. Then imitate a rhythm your friend has clapped for you.

For something more adventurous, try to:

• Clap a short rhythm and have your friend clap it back twice as fast:

(YOU)

(YOUR FRIEND)

• Clap a short rhythm and have your friend clap it back twice as slowly:

You ▭◻◻ ◻◻ ◻◻
Your friend ▭ ◻◻ ▭▭   ▭▭

- Clap a short rhythm and have your friend repeat it, adding another rhythm. Keep adding rhythms until neither of you can repeat the whole thing:

You ▭◻◻ ◻▭ ▭▭

Your friend ▭ ◻◻ ◻▭ ▭▭ ◻◻ ▭◻◻▭

You ▭◻◻ ▭▭ ▭▭ ◻◻ ▭◻◻ ◻▭◻◻◻◻▭

- Clap a short rhythm and have your friend clap it backwards:

You ▭◻◻ ◻▭ ▭▭

Your friend ▭▭ ◻▭▭ ◻◻ ▭

- Clap the rhythm of a song you both know, and have your friend guess what it is.

TAKING NOTES

A.15

Choose a song both you and your friend know. Sing the first *note* (a single sound with only one pitch), have your friend sing the second (following the rhythm of the song), you sing the third, and so on. The trick here is to connect your note with the one before and after it so it sounds like the song instead of separate notes. It helps if you slightly overlap the end of the last note when you start the next. Can you make it sound like only one person is singing?

PAPER CHASE

A.16

What's the softest sound you've ever heard? What's the loudest?

Sometimes we don't bother listening to soft sounds because the loud ones get all our attention. They are easier to hear and usually push other sounds out of the way. Soft and loud also mean different things at different times. A dentist's drill might seem loud when it's inside your mouth, but it isn't loud at all when compared to an airplane engine.

Take a sheet of paper. Try to pass it back and forth between you and another person without making any noise. Remember, any sound you make touching or moving it, tapping or rubbing it—no matter how quiet—counts. These are fragile, tiny sounds, but they are still sounds and not silences.

For something even harder, try passing a page from a newspaper, a sheet of butcher paper, or the largest sheet of paper you can find. Try passing the paper with a group of people. Did you ever think a paper could be this loud?

PAPER MUSIC

How many different sounds can you make with a sheet of paper?

Tear it, rub it, wave it, tap it, crumple it, crease it, blow across it, slap it. Make sounds slowly and quickly, softly and loudly. Do you get the same sounds with different kinds of paper?

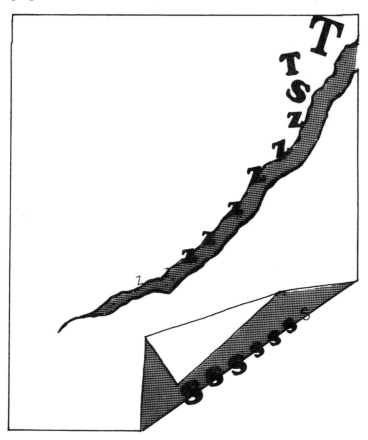

MYSTERY SOUNDS

A.18

Blindfold you friend. Find some ordinary sounds and have your friend guess what they are.

For example: bang coat hangers together, sweep the floor or carpet with a broom, turn on the water faucet (does the hot water sound the same as the cold?), open and close a drawer or cabinet door, open and close the freezer, roll roller skates, lock a lock, zip a zipper, dial a telephone, tear some lettuce, tear off masking tape, open a bag of pretzels, bite into a pickle, or crumple tin foil. Break a piece of chalk, write with it, or scratch it on a chalkboard. Shake a container of salt, a can of peanuts, or a box of cornflakes. Drop a pen and a pencil. Flip some cards, the pages of a book, magazine, or telephone book. Drop a penny, a dime, and a quarter. Can your friend hear the difference?

Have your friend make sounds for you. If you make a mistake, don't worry. We use our eyes so much we often can't tell a sound without them.

TABLE TOP TOUCH

A.19

Sit at a table or on the floor and close your eyes. Ask a friend to put a kitchen timer, portable radio, or other object that makes a sound someplace close to you. Listen, then try to touch the sound. Don't feel around for it. Aim for a direct hit.

FINDING BY SOUND

A.20

Start with a group of friends in the center of the room. Have everyone choose a partner and invent a funny sound both partners can make with their voices. Mix everyone up so they aren't standing close to their partners. When you say "go" have your friends close their eyes, make their sounds, start walking, and find their partners by listening for the sound they agreed on. No peeking!

EYES IN YOUR EARS

A.21

Sit down and close your eyes. Ask a friend to honk a horn or sing a song or make some other sound while walking slowly around the room. Follow the sound by pointing at it with your finger.

There are many different ways to play this game. Have your friend keep clicking a clicker or keep tapping two pieces of wood together (lightly, please!), and:

- Move the sound slowly up and down from your toes to the top of your head. Can you tell when the sound is in front of your nose? In front of your chest?

- Move the sound slowly from left to right or right to left. Stop the sound when you think it is in front of your shoulder. Or in front of your face.
- Move the sound closer and further away, in a straight line in front of you. Can you stop the sound when it's ten feet away? Five feet? Two inches?
- Move the sound in a big circle around you. Stop the sound when it's directly in front, to the right, in back, and to the left of you.
- Walk the following shapes slowly in front of you: circle, triangle, rectangle, square.
- Walk some letters of the alphabet (see illustration). Can you tell what the letter is by listening? Be sure your friend uses plenty of space so you have time to listen.

MONJLSUWYZ

CATCHING
BY SOUND

A.22

You'll need a rubber ball with bells inside for this one. Stand several yards away from a friend, close your eyes, and play a game of "catch" by listening for the ball. Be sure to roll the ball and not throw it. The greater the distance between the two of you, the more time you have to listen.

SOUND SHADOWS
AND TALKING WALLS

A.23

Have you ever listened to a wall talk?
A wall can tell you when you are coming close to it. Stand six to eight feet away from one, and close your eyes. Put one hand a few inches away from your face, palm facing outwards, to protect your nose. Walk very slowly toward the wall and stop when you think the wall is just in front of your hand. Were you able to stop before you touched it? Did you hear or feel anything different?

Just like an object blocking the sun creates a shadow, a large object (like a wall) that blocks sound can also create a shadow. When you are inside this shadow, the object "tells" you it is in the way. You feel the shadow because of a change in air pressure. You hear it because sounds get softer. The color of the sound changes, too, based on the kinds of surfaces around you. (See *Something to Shout About,* *A.7.*)

NO LOOKING
INSIDE

A.24

Blind people always have to see with their ears. Sound shadows, the number of windows and type of furniture in a room, and what the walls and floor are covered with give places a special timbre that helps tell blind people where they are.

Take a short walk with a blindfolded friend inside a building. Ask your friend to tell you where you are or what kind of room you are in. Some places you can try are:

- living rooms with overstuffed furniture, carpets, and drapes
- rooms with hardly anything in them at all
- basements
- lobbies
- staircases (be sure to tell your friend when to step up or down)
- bathrooms
- large, open rooms (auditoriums, cafeterias, gymnasiums)
- hallways

NO LOOKING
OUTSIDE

A.25

Sound shadows, the direction and distance a sound is coming from, and the way a sound moves are some other clues that tell blind people where they are.

Take a blindfolded friend on a short walk outdoors. Try leading your friend:

- Past open spaces (a schoolyard or parking lot), then past a sound shadow (large building or truck). Can your friend guess the size of the object by where the shadow starts and ends?

- Through narrow spaces between buildings.
- Past one way traffic. Can your friend tell you which direction it's going?
- Past an intersection, with traffic moving in two directions.
- Under an overpass or through a tunnel.
- Along a wide avenue or narrow street.
- Into a park. Can your friend tell you how many people are close by, what their ages are, and what they are doing?

PART B:
FACING
THE MUSIC

If you were one of the first people on earth, what kinds of sounds would you hear? Before there were instruments like flutes and tubas and pianos, what would you find to make music with?

Early people used the things closest to them to make music. First, they used themselves. (You can't get much closer than that.) Second, they used the sounds they found in nature. Music was made by using body sounds (like breathing, slapping, and rubbing) and natural objects (like logs, shells, and things that rattled).

Sometimes we can't remember the music we make. Sometimes we want to share our sounds with other people, even if we aren't with them. When this happens, we need to write our music down. In this second part you will discover ways to make music using your body, voice, and the things around you, and some ways to write down what you hear.

LISTEN CLOSELY

B.1

Have you ever put a seashell up to your ear? What you hear isn't the ocean, but the blood rushing through your body.

Put your fingers in your ears. Can you hear your heartbeat and breathing? Can you hear yourself swallow? When you move, can you hear any bones "cracking"? Any high or low pops, or loud or soft clicks?

NATURAL BEAT

Place a hand over your heart. When you feel the two beats, use your other hand to tap out the first (stronger) of the two. This is the beat you feel when you take your pulse. Write it down by drawing a dot for each beat. If the beat is fast, draw the dots close together. If it's slow, draw them further apart.

Discover what someone else's beat is like. Ask them to tap it out while you feel your own. Is their beat the same as yours? Slower? Faster? If you are with a group of friends, ask everyone to tap their beats at the same time ... but be sure you don't start to follow someone else!

AIR TRAINING

Your heart can give you a beat. And your breath can give you a sound.

Blow yourself up like a balloon: First relax, then breathe in slowly, filling your whole body with air. Fill your arms, your legs, your eyes, your head . . . get bigger and taller until you're ready to float away . . . then slowly let the air out with a "hissss." Inflate again. When you have stretched out in all directions imagine someone has pulled out the air hose . . . and the escaping air pushes you clear across the floor with a "phwoosh!" Inflate yourself a third time . . . now, when you are ready to burst, pop the balloon! Don't forget to make a sound when you collapse!

Filling your mouth with "aah": Lay down
on the floor and think about your breathing.
Where does it start? What path does it follow
inside your body?

Breathe in through your nose, press your
lower back against the floor and push your
stomach up to the ceiling, all at the same time.
When you exhale, open your mouth and let the
air out with an "aah" sound. Don't force the
"aah." Let it float on top of your breath.
Breathe in again, and exhale with an "aah,"
this time filling your whole mouth with the
sound. Again . . . filling the whole room with
"aah." Send the sound across the street, then
out for a mile in every direction. Breathe in,
start to exhale, and make faces when you say
"aah." Roll your mouth around: push the
sound up toward your forehead, out to your
right ear, down to your chest, and out to your
left ear.

Things to do with "aah": In the first part of this book, you discovered that your voice (and every other sound) has a *pitch* (high or low quality), timbre (color), and volume (loud or soft quality). It also has a *duration* (length) depending on how much time you take to use it. Here are some ways to say "aah" based on those qualities:

even & straight out: aah_____

wavy: aah∿∿∿

in a whisper: aah__ __ __ __

sliding up: aah_____/

sliding down: aah _____⌐

softly: aah_____

loudly: AAH_____

getting louder & softer: aAh aAh

on different pitches: aah_____
    aah_____
    aah_____

changing pitches by placing hand in front of mouth: aah∿∿∿

short & fast, like a laugh: ahahahahahahah

long & slow: aah aah aah

Harmonizing with "aah": When two or more sounds happen at the same time, the result is called *harmony.* Some harmonies are more pleasant than others. For example, screeching brakes and car horns make a harmony but the harmony of a flute and cello is usually more enjoyable.

Sit or lie down on the floor with one or more friends. Don't plan what you are going to do. Have everyone close their eyes and make sounds with "aah" by themselves. Try some long and slow "aahs" with short and fast ones. Try some sliding up, and some sliding down. Start listening to what everyone else is doing. Do the same thing, or do the opposite. Sing to each other using "aah." Have an argument. Have a conversation. Echo, laugh, get louder, get softer.

Some people have seen beautiful, wet forests or felt like they were floating away while harmonizing with "aah." Did any pictures or feelings come to you while doing the exercise?

RIB TICKLERS

When you fill your mouth with "aah," certain parts of your body vibrate. Which parts of your body do you think vibrate best?

To find out, hum. Push an "m" sound all the way up front in your mouth so you tickle your lips. Touch your teeth together and feel them vibrate. Open your lips a little, and push the sound through your nose. If your nose doesn't tickle when you touch it with your finger, hum on a higher pitch until it does. See if you can vibrate the top of your head by pushing the sound further up, on an even higher pitch. Lower the pitch and rattle your ribs. See if you can vibrate any other parts of your body by changing the pitch.

Different parts will make different sounds depending on their shape and the way they vibrate. The bony parts of your body vibrate better than the fatty parts. Your mouth and nasal passages amplify (strengthen) your voice because of their shape. The shape and kind of wood or metal used to make an instrument helps it sound the way it does, too. Can you imagine the sound a marshmallow drum would make?

ROCK AND ROLL

The way you stand, sit, or move also affects the sounds you make.

Fill your mouth with "aah" and roll your head around. Loosen your neck muscles by dropping your chin to your chest, your right ear to your right shoulder, by lifting your face toward the ceiling, dropping your left ear to your left shoulder, and dropping your chin to your chest again. Does the sound change? Bend from the waist and make circles with your chest like you did with your head. Does this change the sound?

Fill your mouth with "aah." Stretch, press your shoulders down, shake, roll yourself into a ball, rock back and forth, then jump up and down. Twist your spine, stand on your head, lie on your back, lie on your stomach, do somersaults, or run backwards. Feel where the vibrations go and how the sound changes with each activity.

BODY SOUNDS
CATALOG

Before there were violins and guitars, people made all kinds of music just by using their bodies. You can make body sounds by:

- *rubbing*—parts of your body together, hands together, hands against the floor, your whole foot back and forth against the floor, your toes, then heels, against the floor
- *slapping*—with open hands against your chest, thighs, back, buttocks, stomach, other body parts and objects
- *snapping*—fingers (some people can snap their toes!)
- *tapping*—with fingertips, nails, heels or toes against different objects

- *popping*—knuckles and toes (but don't do it too often)
- *stomping*—feet flat against the floor
- *clicking*—nails against each other
- *clapping*—your own hands together or against someone else's hands

Although these sounds don't have a pitch you can sing, some are higher or lower than others. You can change them even more by doing them faster or slower, or louder or softer.

Some sounds you can make with your mouth, but not with your voice, are:

- *clicking*—your teeth together (lightly, so you don't loosen any fillings), clicking the tip, one side, or both sides of your tongue against the top of your mouth, sides of your mouth, or against your teeth
- *fluttering*—your tongue, tongue against the soft palate (the roof of your mouth), fluttering your throat (like a gargle) or lips (like a motorboat)

- *smacking*—your lips (like a kiss)
- *popping*—your lips, or cheeks (by puffing them up and popping your finger in and out of your mouth), popping by slapping or tapping your puffed-up cheeks, or by driving out pockets of air with your tongue
- *plopping*—your tongue loosely against the bottom of your mouth
- *squishing*—liquid in your mouth (mouth closed, or carefully with lips open)

Some sounds you can make with your breath are:
- *hissing*
- *whistling*
- *pushing* air around the sides of your tongue (like Donald Duck), under your tongue (like a Bronx cheer), or through your lips
- *whispering*
- *coughing* (without your voice)

You can change the pitch, volume, and timbre of mouth and breath sounds by:
- *changing the shape* of your mouth
- *changing the position* of your tongue
- *changing the amount of air pressure* you use
- *tensing and relaxing* muscles
- *opening or closing* your mouth
- *closing off* the back of your mouth with your tongue (the normal place for your tongue when you breathe through your nose)

Tap dancing is one body sound that is still used today. Can you think of any others?

Things to do with body sounds: Give a body sound a *beat* (a steady, repeated pulse). Make the sound a few times, then have a friend imitate it. Be sure your friend copies the exact speed of your beat and volume of your sound. Then imitate a sound your friend makes.

Perform a body sound once. Have your friend repeat it and quickly do a new one. Repeat your friend's sound, and change it to another. Keep going back and forth. The less you think about what you are doing, the more surprising the sounds will be.

Ask a question using two body sounds. For example, pop your lips and clap your hands three times (pop,clap/pop,clap/pop,clap). Have your friend "answer" it three times with a new pair of sounds (for example, by hissing then tapping toes—hiss,tap/hiss,tap/hiss,tap). The faster your friend answers, the more of a beat you'll get. Imagine your friend's answer is now the question, and answer it three times with two more sounds. Keep going back and forth.

ORCHESTRA

B.7

A *conductor* helps an orchestra play to-gether. The conductor does this by listening to what everyone is doing. The orchestra must watch the conductor for *cues* (when to start)

and *cut offs* (when to stop). Everyone has to cooperate for the music to sound good.

To create an orchestra, you'll need a few friends—the more, the better! Ask each person to choose a body sound they can easily repeat. As the leader (conductor), you tell people when and how to make their sounds. To start someone, point. To stop them, turn your hand quickly to the right (if you are right handed) or left (if you are left handed). To get a louder sound, move both hands away from the sides of your body like you were stretching a rubber band. To get a softer sound, do the opposite (bring your hands closer together). If you want to get really fancy, use both hands to conduct two different parts at once. Or hold a dull pencil in one hand as a *baton* (that small stick you've seen conductors point with).

Listen carefully to the sounds your orchestra is making. You might want to combine similar sounds, or combine different ones. Some sounds can be short, and some long. You might want to give a sound a beat, have questions and answers between sounds (see page 56), or have only two sounds happen at once to create harmony.

RAIN DANCE

Early people didn't make music just for fun.
They used music to tell stories, send messages,
and to make things happen—just by imitating
them.

Use your body sounds orchestra to create a
rainstorm. Start with a light rainfall by having everyone tap their fingers or fingernails
slowly against the floor. Make the rainfall
heavier by clapping lightly... then stronger
by slapping your thighs... and heavier by
slapping your chests... and heavier still by
slapping the floor. Lighten the storm to a
drippy finish by using tongue clicks and lip
pops. If it rains within 24 hours, try for snow.

SEE WHAT YOU HEAR
B.9

A *found sound* is a sound made by nature or by an object you find around you.

The sounds we find around us today are different from the sounds the earliest people found. We can still hear the rain, birds, insects, and animals, but we also hear cars, trains, radios, and machines. The sounds of traffic or a siren have become as natural to our lives as the sounds of a waterfall were to the first people on earth. Just like people used the sounds of nature to make music in the past, the sounds that are natural to us can be used to make music today.

Find objects inside your home or school that can make sounds. Don't choose ones that are already used for music, like bells or drums. Choose objects you never thought of making music with before.

Depending on how you turn a pencil sharpener, you hear a continuous grinding sound that slows down and speeds up. If you press a stapler, you hear short clicks: one or two when the top hits the bottom, a click when the staple is folded, and a final click when the top pops up. Every sound has a different color, volume, and pitch. The more carefully you listen, the more you'll hear.

Choose one found sound you like and invent a way of writing it, not by drawing a picture of the object but of the *sound* it makes. Sometimes it helps if you draw the way the sound moves. For example, shake a can with small objects inside. Then shake a pencil on the paper like you were still shaking the can. What you see might look something like this:

The sound goes all over the place, and so does the picture.

Or drop a pencil on the floor. The sound starts slowly, then speeds up. The pencil drops, bounces, stops, bounces again, then bounces faster and faster until it stops. Move

your hand with the sound and you might see
something like this:

When you turn a pencil sharpener, your
hand moves around in a circle. When you use a
stapler, your hand moves up and down. When
you use a pair of scissors, your hand opens and
closes, and when you riffle the pages of a book,
your finger moves in an arc.

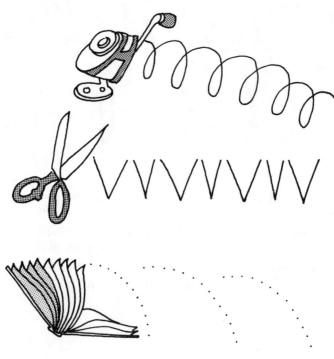

Things to do with found sounds: Draw a soundshape. First, put a few found sounds next to each other. Then number the sounds across the top of a sheet of paper. Draw a dot to show the pitch, from high to low, of each sound. Connect the dots to see their shape. Draw shapes for other sounds. If you have trouble finding sounds, choose some from your journal or from the list of mystery sounds (A.18).

Or, make a musical scene. Listen to all the sounds around you like you did with *Far and Near* (A.1).To create a musical landscape, draw a picture of each sound, putting high sounds near the top of the page and low ones near the bottom. Draw scenes for other places.

PEN CLICK
JIGGLING COINS
TALKING
SNEEZE
TALKING (WITH LAUGH)
BANGING A CARTON
WALKING

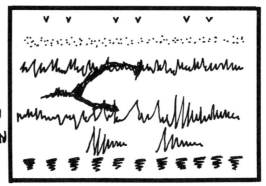

FOUND SOUNDS
ORCHESTRA

When you improvise music (create it on the spot), you can't always repeat it. If you write music down you have more control over what happens, and can always remember it.

On a sheet of paper, mark down eight of your heartbeats across the top, and number them 1 to 8. Each beat will equal one count. The closer together you draw the beats, the faster your count will go.

Choose two found sounds and decide how to write them. One object will be the first instrument of your orchestra (written on top), the other, the second instrument of your orchestra (written below):

HEARTBEATS

CAN OF PENCILS   PENCIL SHARPENER

As you count to 8, when do you want to hear the first instrument? For the first four counts? The second four counts? All eight counts? Some other way?

As you count to 8, when do you want to hear the second sound? Do you want to hear it together with the first sound? Sometimes with it, and sometimes without it? You might want to change the first part as you work with the second.

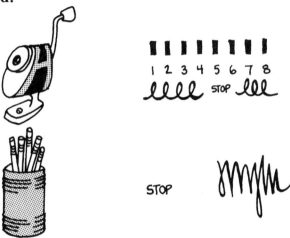

Ask a friend to help you play your composition. Does it sound like you expected it to? Would you like to change anything? Repeat your piece two or three times in a row so you can really feel the beat and hear the way the two instruments work together.

Most found sounds and body sounds are *percussive* sounds, made by hitting or shaking objects together. Can your find any sounds to use that are made by blowing across or through an object?

DRASTIC MEASURES

Compose another piece for two found sounds, using different instruments. This time, mark 16 counts (beats) instead of 8. Don't worry about how close together you draw the beats. Separate every four beats with a vertical line (called a *bar line*), and put two lines at the end (one thin and one thick) so you know it's the last beat. The distance between bar lines is called a *measure*. Measures make it easier for you and your friend to see each part, and know when to play it.

On which of the 16 counts do you want the first instrument to sound?

1 2 3 4	5 6 7 8	9 10 11 12	13 14 15 16
measure	measure	measure	measure

DOUBLE BAR LINE

INSIDE THE CLOSET

BANGING COAT HANGERS (in a closet)

FAST

1 2 3 4	5 6 7 8	9 10 11 12	13 14 15 16

HITTING SHOE AGAINST FLOOR

On which of the 16 counts do you want the second instrument to sound? Listen carefully to the pitch and timbre of each instrument, and how they sound together. This will help you decide when to write them. You might want to think of the first 8 beats as a "question," and the second 8 beats as an "answer."

How loud do you want the sounds to be? How soft? Sometimes loud and sometimes soft? Louder, then softer? If one of your sounds is naturally louder than the other, you might have to play it softly so the other can be heard. Use dark or large lines and shapes for loud sounds. Use light or small lines and shapes for soft ones. You might even want to have one or two beats that are louder than the rest.

Do you want the *tempo* (speed) to be slow, medium, or fast? Over the first measure write the word "Quickly" or "Slowly" or whatever speed you want.

Compose a third piece, for soft, tiny sounds, using 12 beats. Separate every three beats with a bar line and put two bar lines at the end.

Be sure to give your pieces titles. You might even refer to some music you've already heard:

The Aching 12 Overture (for "oos" and "aahs")
Sweeping Beauty (for brooms)
Pitchers at an Exhibition (for different sized
    pitchers)
The Eggmount Overture (for eggslicers)
Beethoven's Fifth (bottle symphony)

TALKING
WITHOUT WORDS

B.12

Before there were alphabets or words, people used vocal sounds to tell each other how they felt.

How do you feel right now? Forget that you can talk. Take a breath and let out a sound—not a word—that sounds like how you feel. If there is someone else around, find out how they are feeling.

SOUND TOSS

Make a vocal sound, and send it through the air to a friend. Use your whole body to help. Have your friend "catch" the sound using his or her hands, then toss a new sound to you. Did the sound break? Scatter? Float? Crumble? Evaporate? Can you see its color and size? Can you feel its temperature, texture, and weight?

PAINT
WITH YOUR VOICE

B.14

We are used to seeing pictures with our eyes. Sometimes we forget that our voices can also make pictures.

Use your voice to:
- blow out a candle
- stampede an elephant
- seduce a spider
- direct traffic
- raise the dead
- kiss
- tickle a whale
- pet a porcupine
- chisel a statue
- paint a cloud
- comb your hair
- put yourself to sleep
- knock a hole in a wall
- blow over a chair
- crack an egg
- roll an egg
- push someone
- sweep the floor
- inflate a zeppelin
- create a bubble of sound around yourself that gets bigger and smaller
- warm a castle
- stop time

Send your voice through:
- a wide tunnel
- a narrow tunnel
- an electric fan
- a radiator
- water

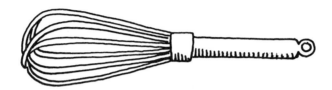

Use your voice as:
- an axe
- a hammer hitting mud
- a pair of tweezers
- scissors cutting through corrugated cardboard
- a red balloon
- a fluorescent light
- barbed wire
- a vegetable
- a wire whisk
- pink cotton candy
- a sponge
- a neon sign
- a walnut
- a beard
- a warm quilt
- a bad odor
- a cigarette ash falling on the floor
- light coming through a stained glass window

LANDSCAPES

B.15

Draw the rooftops of your block. Or the sky-
line of a city. Or draw your path from home to
school. Follow the line with your voice, and
sing what you see.

COOKING EGGS
WITH YOUR MOUTH

B.16

Sometimes music tells a story or describes an event.

Tell a story, just by using vocal sounds. For example: Sound the alarm clock. Turn on the water, brush your teeth, and gargle. Walk to the kitchen, open, then close the refrigerator. Crack eggs and fry them. Pour juice from a bottle, and set the kitchen timer. Miss the bell while you practice the drums. Hear the smoke alarm, pour water over the pan, and run out the door.

VOCAL SOUNDS
CHORUS

B.17

This works just like the body sounds orchestra (B.7), except that the types of sounds are different.

If you have enough people, divide the group into two or three sections, each with its own vocal sound. Otherwise, have each person choose a different sound to perform. Vary the pitches, rhythms, volumes, harmonies, and tempos to create all kinds of *textures* and moods. You can make your music more dramatic by speeding things up, stopping and

starting sounds, adding sounds, or making sounds louder at different times. You can make the music more relaxed by slowing it down, using fewer voices, or making sounds softer. These are also good ways to end your piece.

Things to do with a vocal sounds chorus: Decide on a theme like "traffic," "bubble bath," "machines," or "how you feel." Conduct the chorus, having each person or section choose a sound based on the theme. Members of the chorus might want to move like the sounds they are making.

Conduct a nature concert. Have each section of the chorus choose a sound related to a theme like birds (pigeon coos, chicken clucks, and fluttering wings), swamps, wild animals, or forests (waterfalls, babbling brooks, crunching leaves, and breaking twigs).

Perform a symphony by imitating sounds you would hear around your house (food cooking, doors creaking, dishwashers washing, vacuum cleaners humming, bottles filling, doorbells ringing).

Draw a map of a room and label different areas with different vocal sounds. Using your map as a guide, place members of the chorus in different areas and conduct them. Keep the map in front of you so you can see what everyone is doing. For this activity, if there are several people in a section, they don't all have to do exactly the same thing. Each person can make whatever sound he or she feels matches the label.

If you can round up enough friends, have two conductors lead two choruses at the same time. This is a bit like *Double Talk* (A.12): conductors should listen to what each other's chorus is doing while they are listening to their own. That way they can relate sounds back and forth. If conductors experiment with all the elements of sound, the possibilities for textures are endless.

MAD **MAD** **MAD** MAD

REPEATING
YOURSELF

B.18

Grunts, groans, and swampy sounds eventually became words. And every word is a tiny musical composition, when you know how to listen to it.

Choose a word with a strong feeling or emotion. It could be a word like mad, happy, sad, or bored. Or a word like ugly, lovely, curvy, or stop. Repeat the word three or four times. Each time you say it, make the word sound more like what it means.

Some words sound more like their meanings than others. Choose a word that already sounds like what it means (like "bubbly"—with all those b's), and repeat it three or four times, each time making it sound more like its meaning.

Choose a word that doesn't really sound like what it means (like "sneeze") and invent a new word for it that does.

REPEAT YOURSELF
AGAIN

Repeat the same word thirty times in thirty different ways. If you get stuck, use some of the ideas in B.23 to help. When you finish, find five more!

TONGUE TWISTERS

Say the following tongue twisters fast, three times in a row. Listen carefully to the sound each one makes, and the way it feels in your mouth. Concentrate on the way one sound leads to another, and the way you have to move your mouth to get it there.

- Black bug's blood.
- The sixth sheik's sixth sheep's sick.
- The seething sea ceaseth, and thus the seething sea sufficeth us.
- Lemon liniment.
- Peggy Babcock.

Listen to the special timbre and rhythm of these twisters:

- A noisy noise annoys an oyster.
- A critical cricket critic.
- Which witch has the Swiss wristwatch?
- How many cans As many cans
  Can a canner can As a canner can
  If a canner If a canner
  Can can cans? Can can cans.
  A canner can can